GRAPHIC HISTORY

THE MYSTERY OF THE Roanoke COLONY

by Xavier Niz

illustrated by Shannon Eric Denton

Consultant:
Dr. E. Thomson Shields Jr., Director
Roanoke Colonies Research Office
East Carolina University
Greenville, N.C.

Capstone press

Mankato, Minnesota

Graphic Library is published by Capstone Press,
1710 Roe Crest Drive, North Mankato, Minnesota 56003.
www.capstonepub.com

Library of Congress Cataloging-in-Publication Data
Niz, Xavier.
　The mystery of the Roanoke Colony / by Xavier Niz; illustrated by Shannon Eric Denton.
　p. cm.—(Graphic library. Graphic history)
　Summary: "In graphic novel format, tells the mysterious story of the disappearance of a
group of early American colonists"—Provided by publisher.
　Includes bibliographical references and index.
　ISBN-13: 978-0-7368-6494-7 (hardcover)
　ISBN-10: 0-7368-6494-6 (hardcover)
　ISBN-13: 978-0-7368-9657-3 (softcover pbk.)
　ISBN-10: 0-7368-9657-0 (softcover pbk.)
　1. Roanoke Colony—Juvenile literature. 2. Roanoke Island (N.C.)—History—16th century—
Juvenile literature. I. Denton, Shannon Eric. II. Title. III. Series.
F229.N59 2007
975.6'175—dc22   2006007791

Graphic Designers
Jason Knudson and Kim Brown

Colorist
Kristen Fitzner Denton

Editor
Martha E. H. Rustad

Printed in the United States   5914

Table of Contents

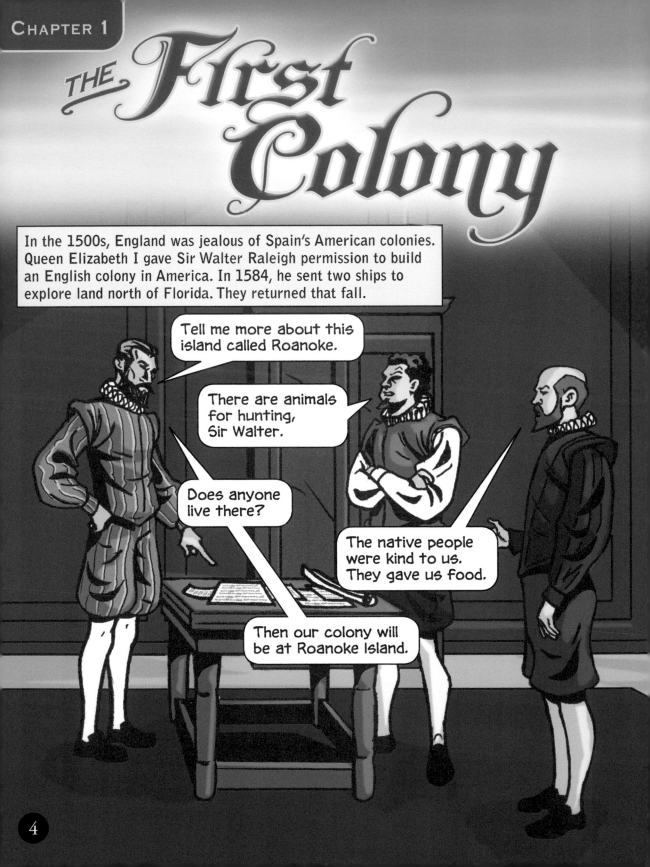

CHAPTER 1

THE First Colony

In the 1500s, England was jealous of Spain's American colonies. Queen Elizabeth I gave Sir Walter Raleigh permission to build an English colony in America. In 1584, he sent two ships to explore land north of Florida. They returned that fall.

Tell me more about this island called Roanoke.

There are animals for hunting, Sir Walter.

Does anyone live there?

The native people were kind to us. They gave us food.

Then our colony will be at Roanoke Island.

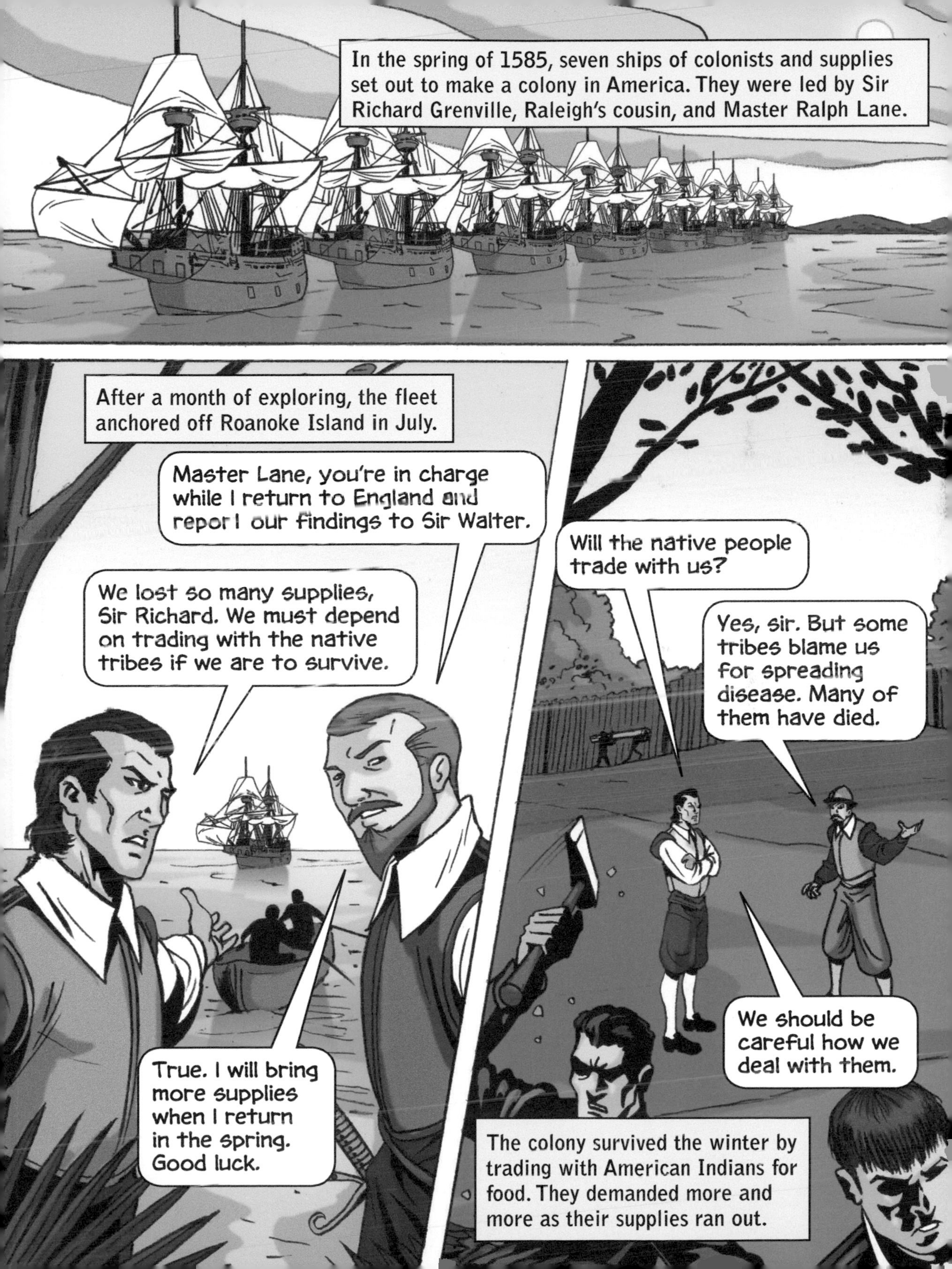
In the spring of 1585, seven ships of colonists and supplies set out to make a colony in America. They were led by Sir Richard Grenville, Raleigh's cousin, and Master Ralph Lane.
After a month of exploring, the fleet anchored off Roanoke Island in July.
Master Lane, you're in charge while I return to England and report our findings to Sir Walter.
We lost so many supplies, Sir Richard. We must depend on trading with the native tribes if we are to survive.
True. I will bring more supplies when I return in the spring. Good luck.
Will the native people trade with us?
Yes, sir. But some tribes blame us for spreading disease. Many of them have died.
We should be careful how we deal with them.
The colony survived the winter by trading with American Indians for food. They demanded more and more as their supplies ran out.

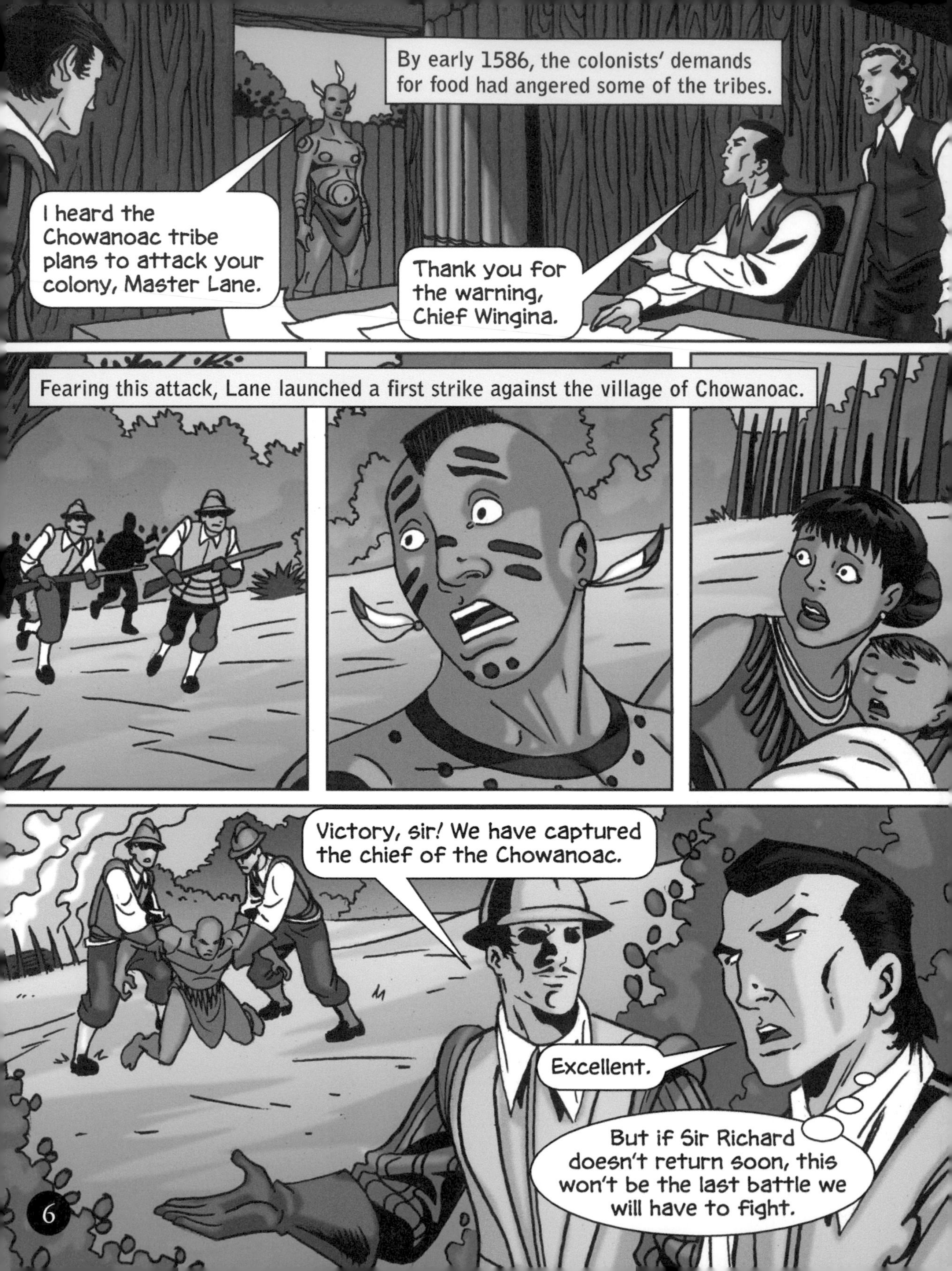

By early 1586, the colonists' demands for food had angered some of the tribes.
I heard the Chowanoac tribe plans to attack your colony, Master Lane.
Thank you for the warning, Chief Wingina.
Fearing this attack, Lane launched a first strike against the village of Chowanoac.
Victory, sir! We have captured the chief of the Chowanoac.
Excellent.
But if Sir Richard doesn't return soon, this won't be the last battle we will have to fight.

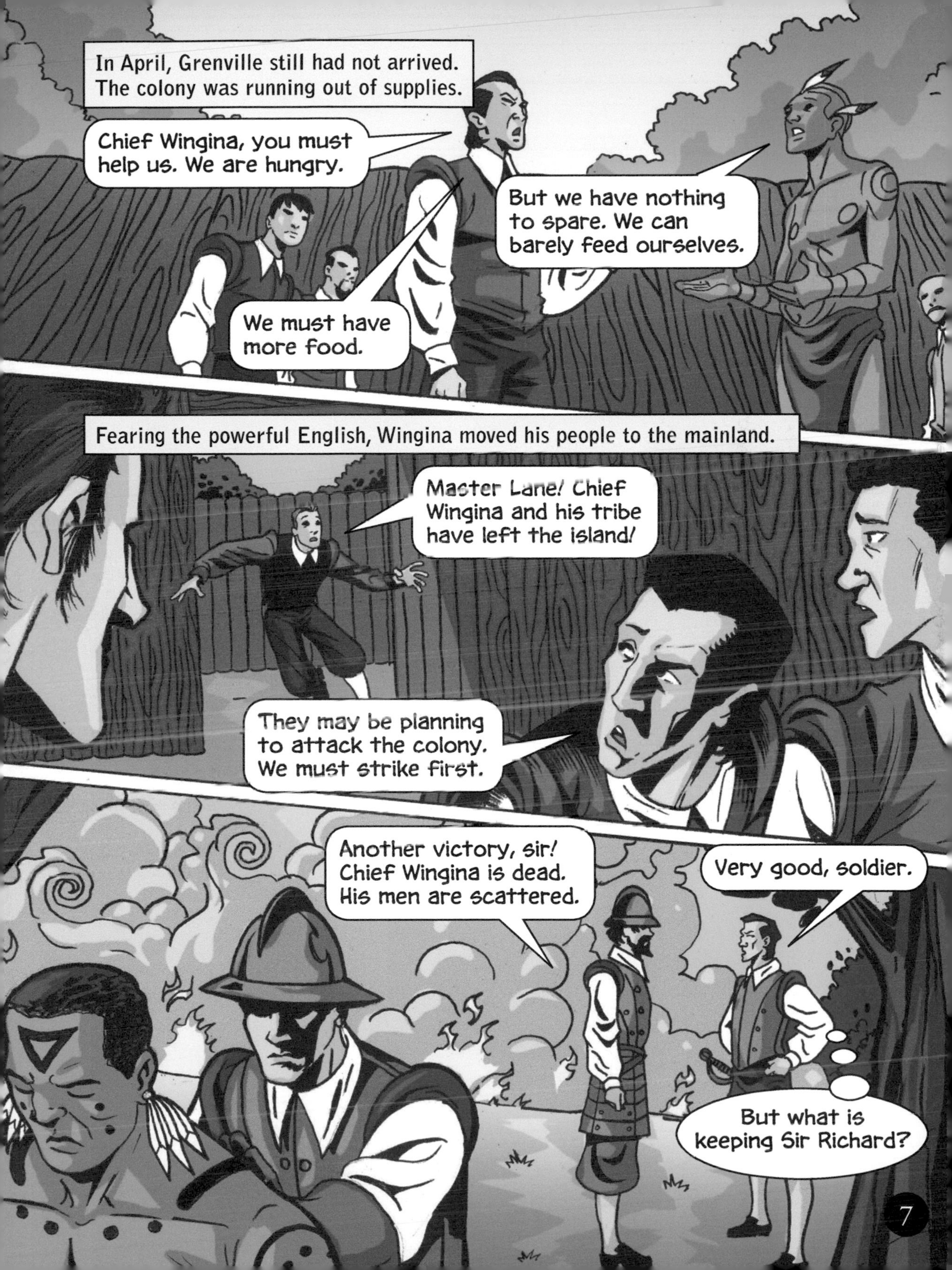

In April, Grenville still had not arrived. The colony was running out of supplies.
Chief Wingina, you must help us. We are hungry.
We must have more food.
But we have nothing to spare. We can barely feed ourselves.
Fearing the powerful English, Wingina moved his people to the mainland.
Master Lane! Chief Wingina and his tribe have left the island!
They may be planning to attack the colony. We must strike first.
Another victory, sir! Chief Wingina is dead. His men are scattered.
Very good, soldier.
But what is keeping Sir Richard?

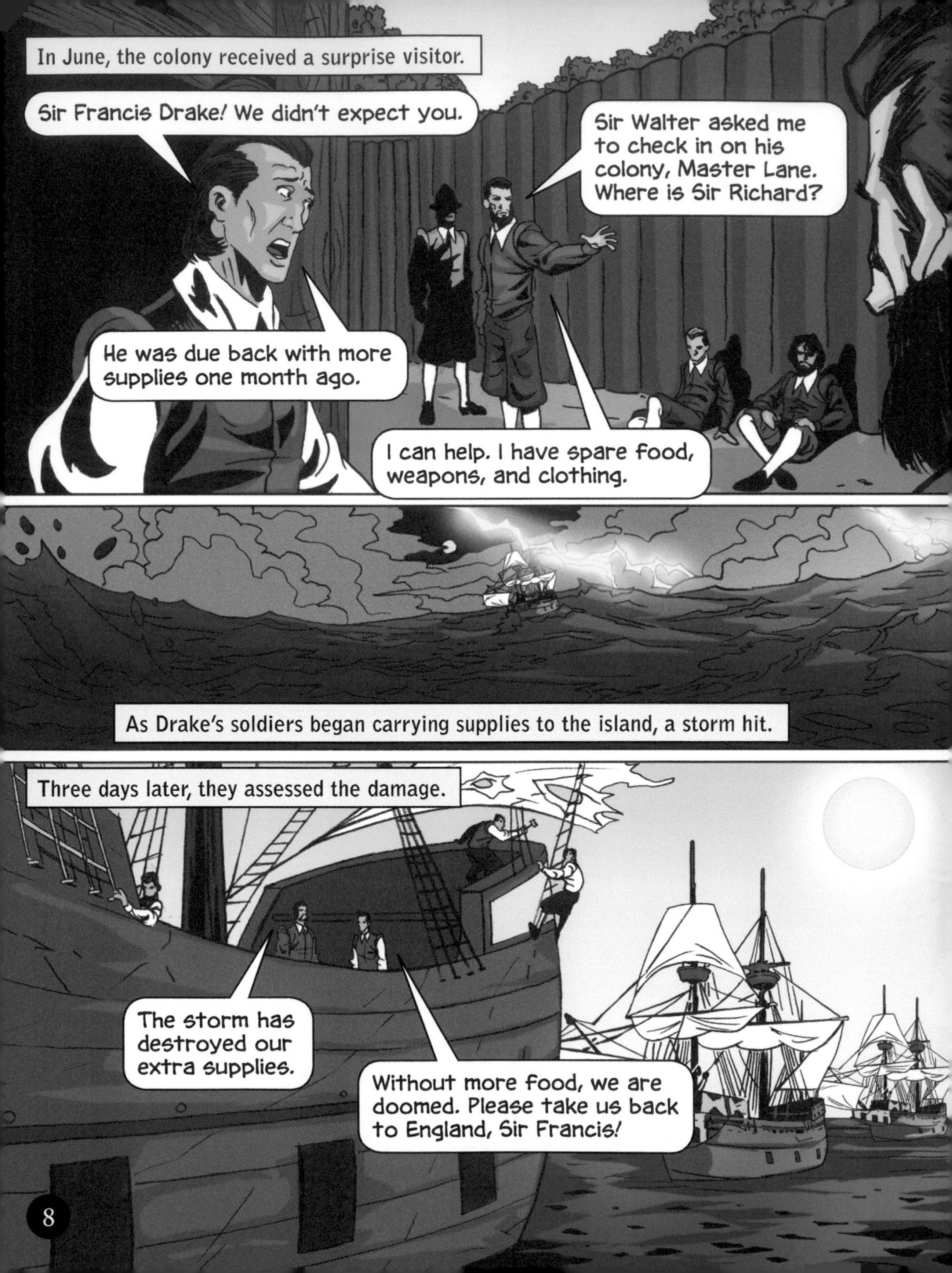
In June, the colony received a surprise visitor.
Sir Francis Drake! We didn't expect you.
Sir Walter asked me to check in on his colony, Master Lane. Where is Sir Richard?
He was due back with more supplies one month ago.
I can help. I have spare food, weapons, and clothing.
As Drake's soldiers began carrying supplies to the island, a storm hit.
Three days later, they assessed the damage.
The storm has destroyed our extra supplies.
Without more food, we are doomed. Please take us back to England, Sir Francis!

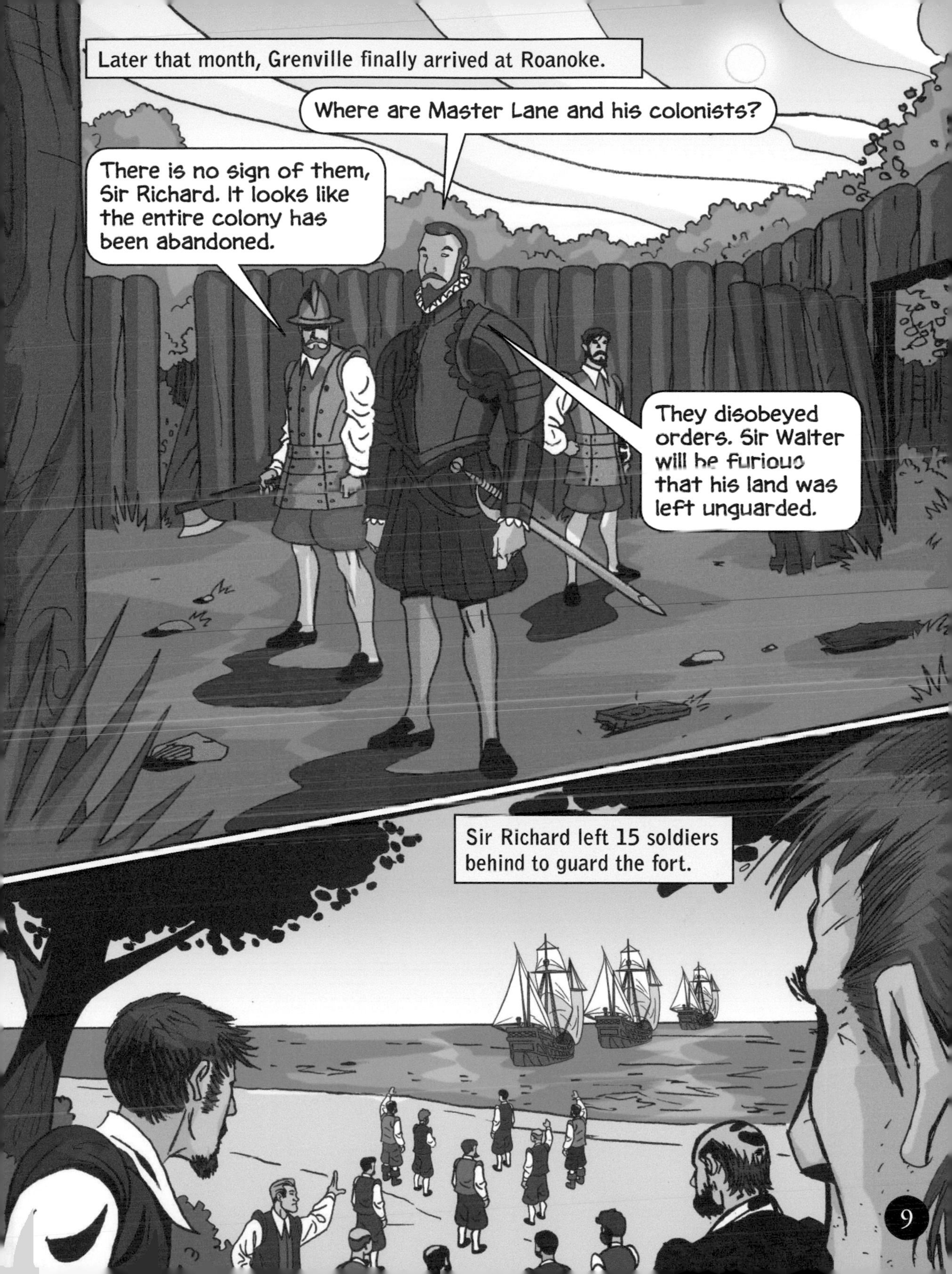
Later that month, Grenville finally arrived at Roanoke.
Where are Master Lane and his colonists?
There is no sign of them, Sir Richard. It looks like the entire colony has been abandoned.
They disobeyed orders. Sir Walter will be furious that his land was left unguarded.
Sir Richard left 15 soldiers behind to guard the fort.

CHAPTER 2

The Second Colony

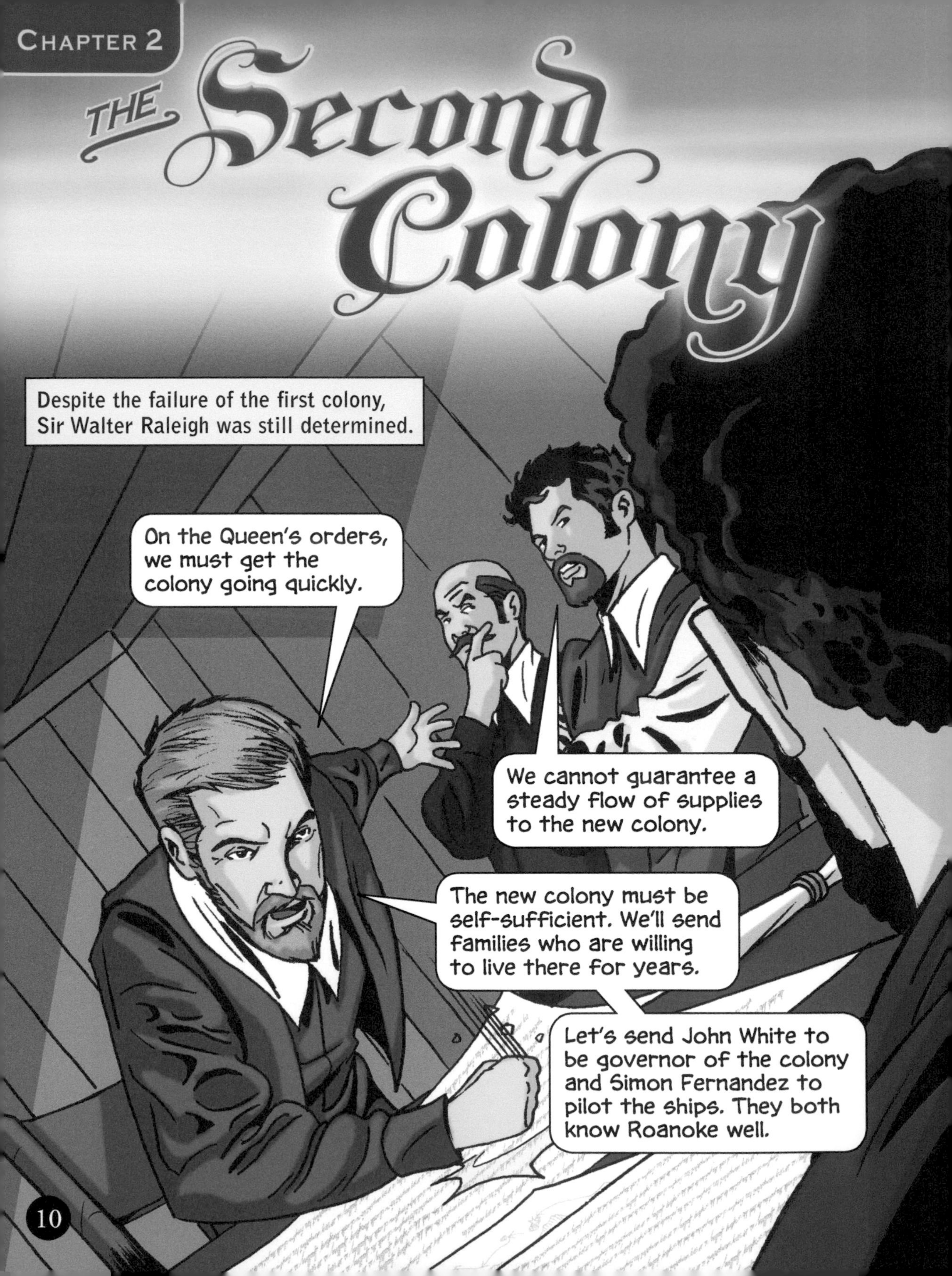
Despite the failure of the first colony, Sir Walter Raleigh was still determined.
On the Queen's orders, we must get the colony going quickly.
We cannot guarantee a steady flow of supplies to the new colony.
The new colony must be self-sufficient. We'll send families who are willing to live there for years.
Let's send John White to be governor of the colony and Simon Fernandez to pilot the ships. They both know Roanoke well.

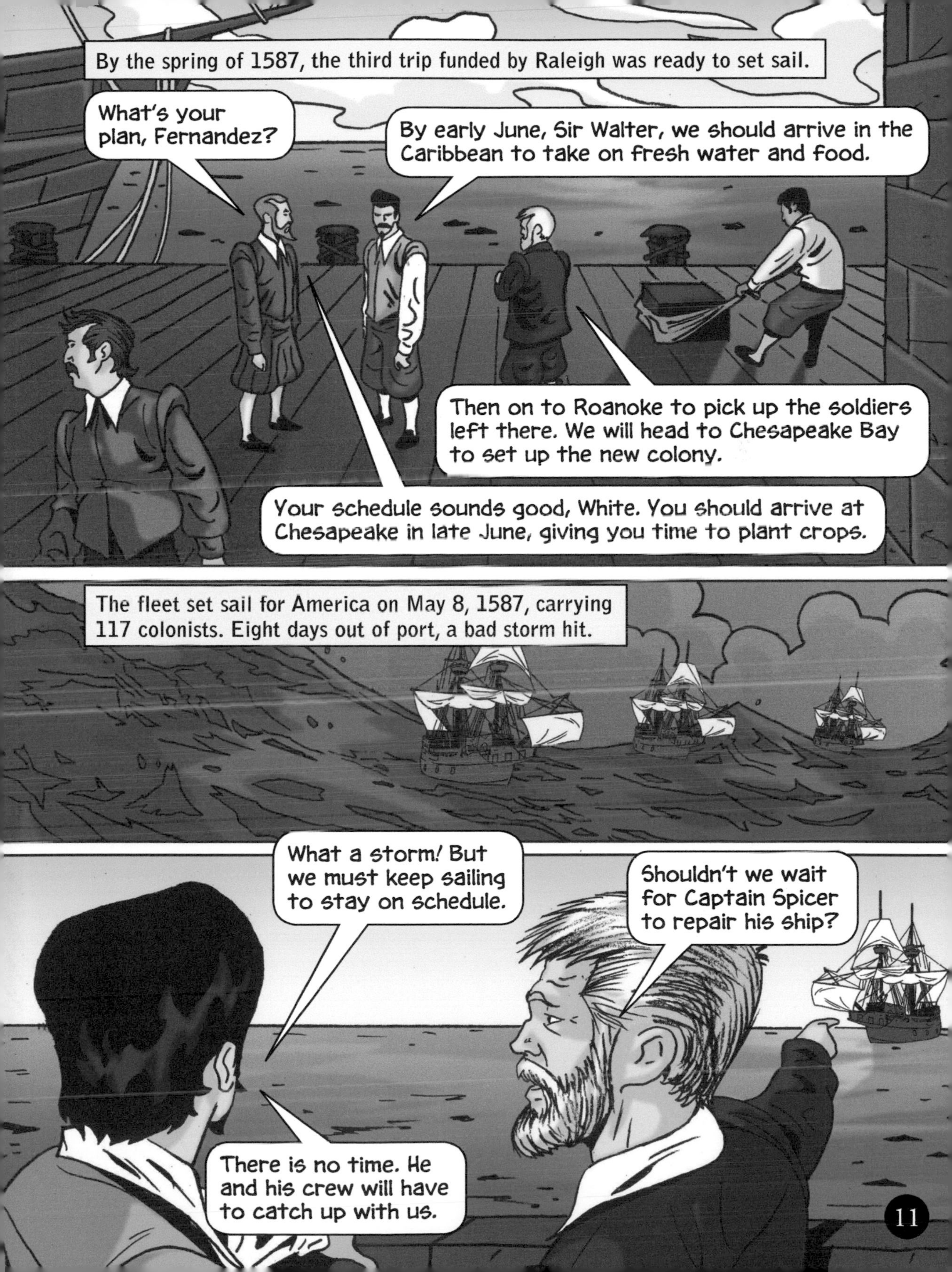
By the spring of 1587, the third trip funded by Raleigh was ready to set sail.
What's your plan, Fernandez?
By early June, Sir Walter, we should arrive in the Caribbean to take on fresh water and food.
Then on to Roanoke to pick up the soldiers left there. We will head to Chesapeake Bay to set up the new colony.
Your schedule sounds good, White. You should arrive at Chesapeake in late June, giving you time to plant crops.
The fleet set sail for America on May 8, 1587, carrying 117 colonists. Eight days out of port, a bad storm hit.
What a storm! But we must keep sailing to stay on schedule.
Shouldn't we wait for Captain Spicer to repair his ship?
There is no time. He and his crew will have to catch up with us.

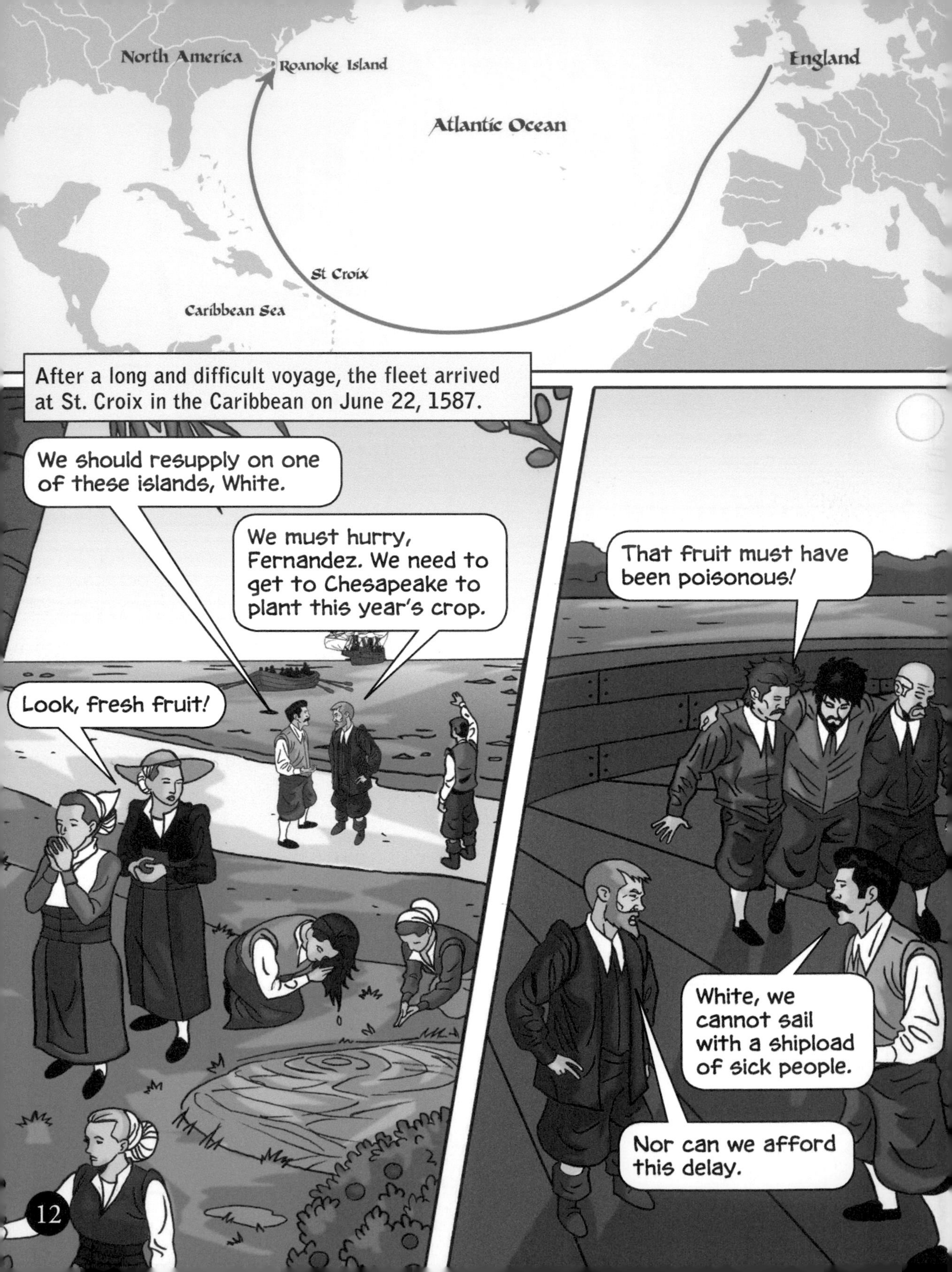
North America
Roanoke Island
England
Atlantic Ocean
St Croix
Caribbean Sea
After a long and difficult voyage, the fleet arrived at St. Croix in the Caribbean on June 22, 1587.
We should resupply on one of these islands, White.
We must hurry, Fernandez. We need to get to Chesapeake to plant this year's crop.
Look, fresh fruit!
That fruit must have been poisonous!
White, we cannot sail with a shipload of sick people.
Nor can we afford this delay.

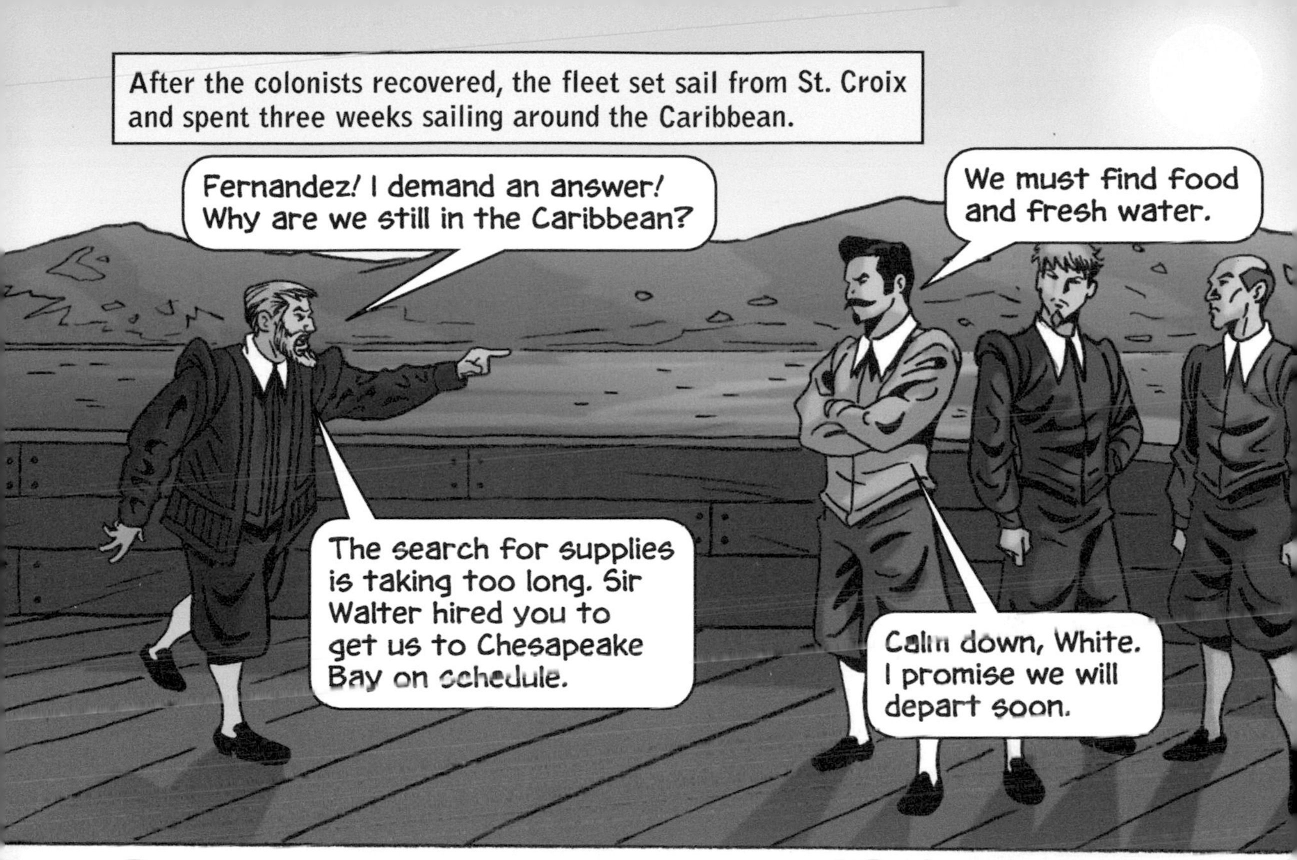
After the colonists recovered, the fleet set sail from St. Croix and spent three weeks sailing around the Caribbean.
Fernandez! I demand an answer! Why are we still in the Caribbean?
We must find food and fresh water.
The search for supplies is taking too long. Sir Walter hired you to get us to Chesapeake Bay on schedule.
Calm down, White. I promise we will depart soon.

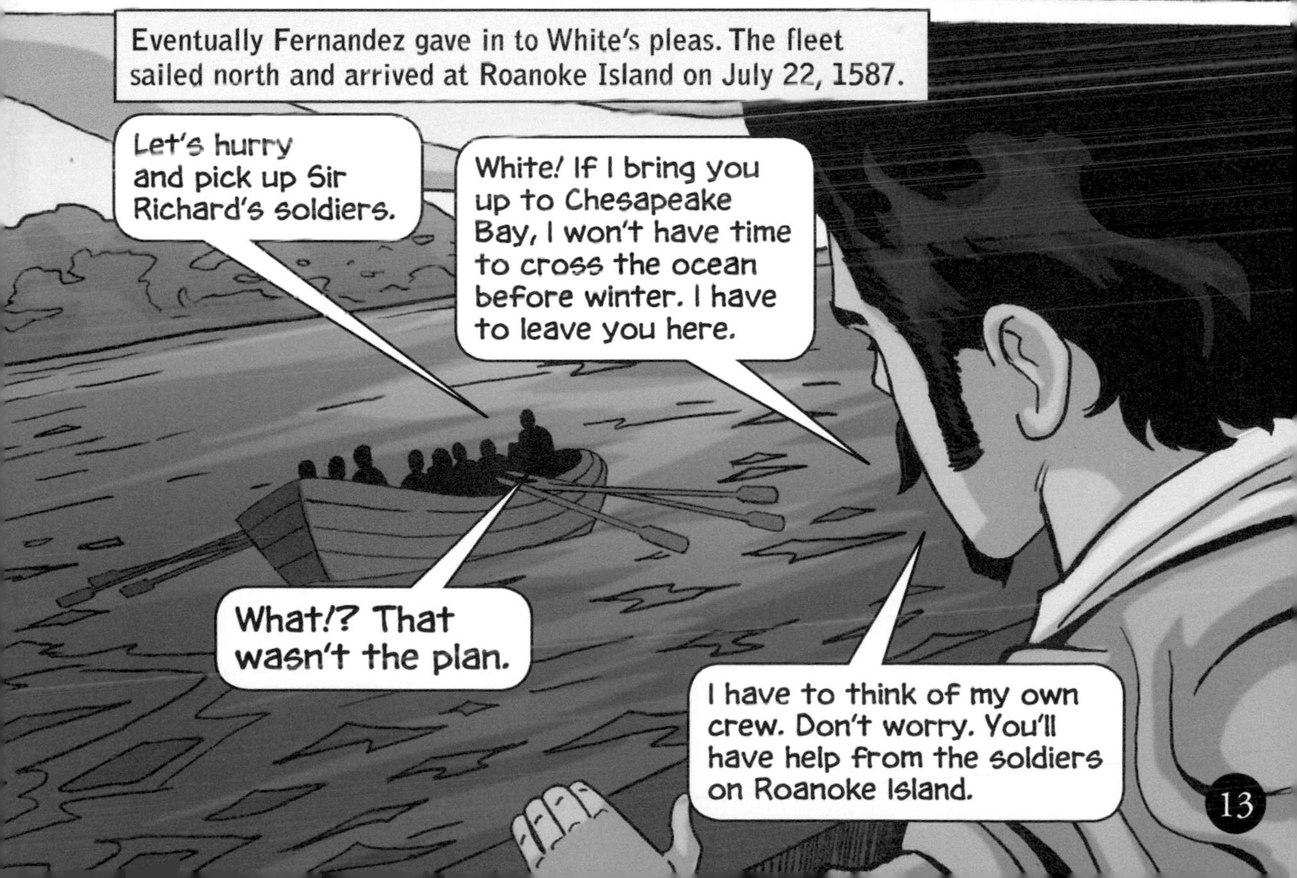
Eventually Fernandez gave in to White's pleas. The fleet sailed north and arrived at Roanoke Island on July 22, 1587.
Let's hurry and pick up Sir Richard's soldiers.
White! If I bring you up to Chesapeake Bay, I won't have time to cross the ocean before winter. I have to leave you here.
What!? That wasn't the plan.
I have to think of my own crew. Don't worry. You'll have help from the soldiers on Roanoke Island.

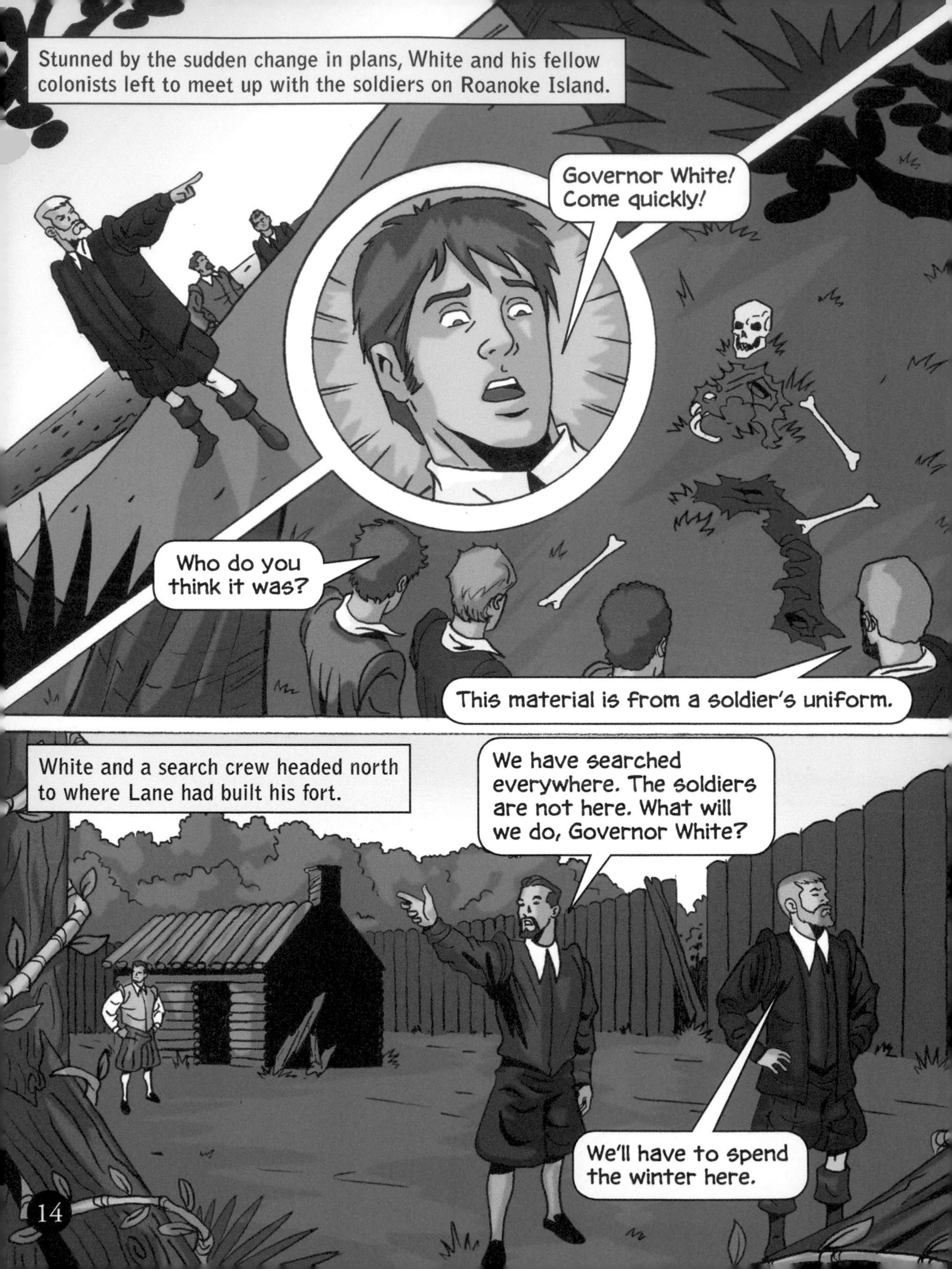
Stunned by the sudden change in plans, White and his fellow colonists left to meet up with the soldiers on Roanoke Island.
Governor White! Come quickly!
Who do you think it was?
This material is from a soldier's uniform.
White and a search crew headed north to where Lane had built his fort.
We have searched everywhere. The soldiers are not here. What will we do, Governor White?
We'll have to spend the winter here.

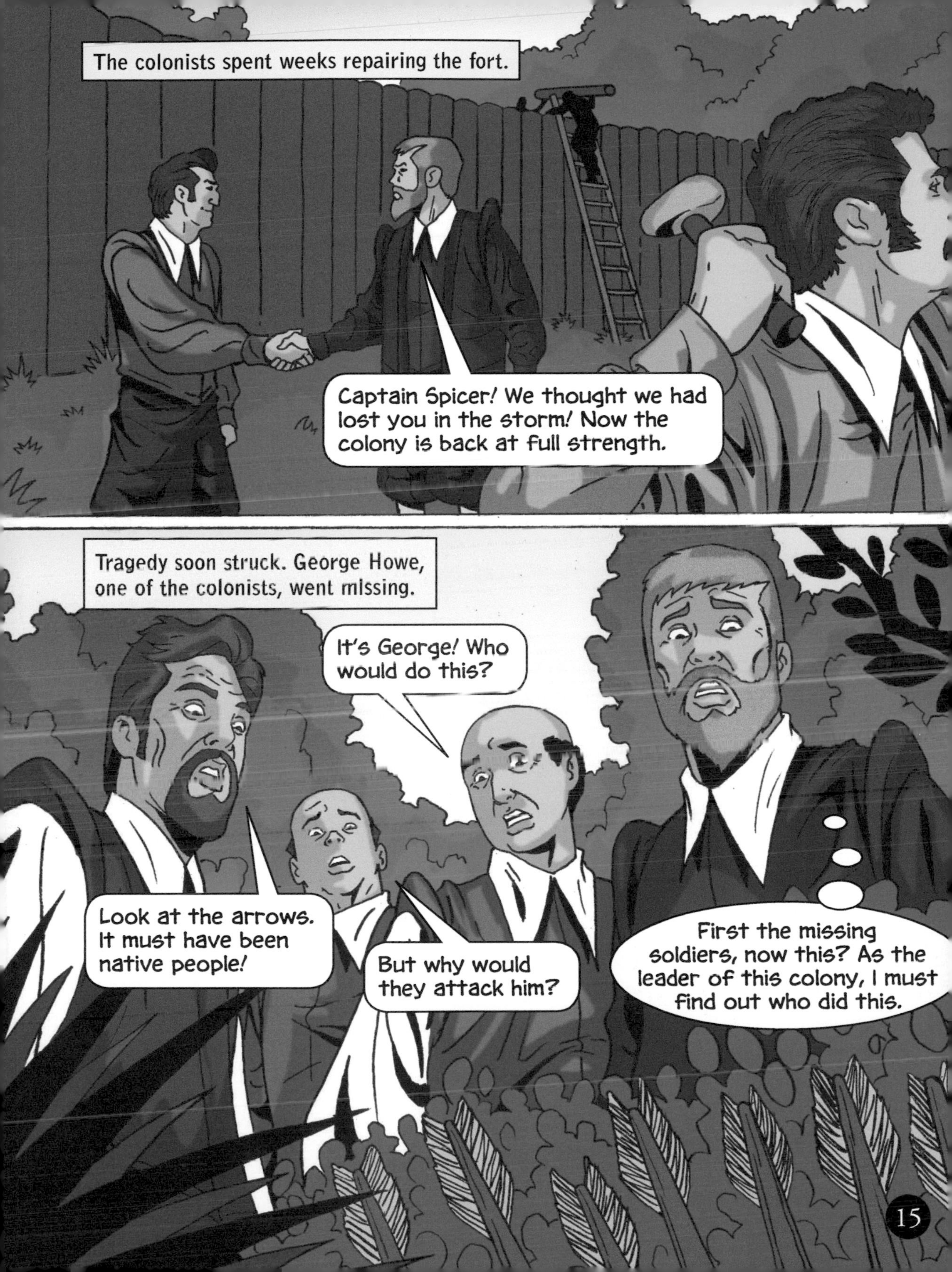

The colonists spent weeks repairing the fort.
Captain Spicer! We thought we had lost you in the storm! Now the colony is back at full strength.
Tragedy soon struck. George Howe, one of the colonists, went missing.
It's George! Who would do this?
Look at the arrows. It must have been native people!
But why would they attack him?
First the missing soldiers, now this? As the leader of this colony, I must find out who did this.

Chapter 3

A Colony in Peril

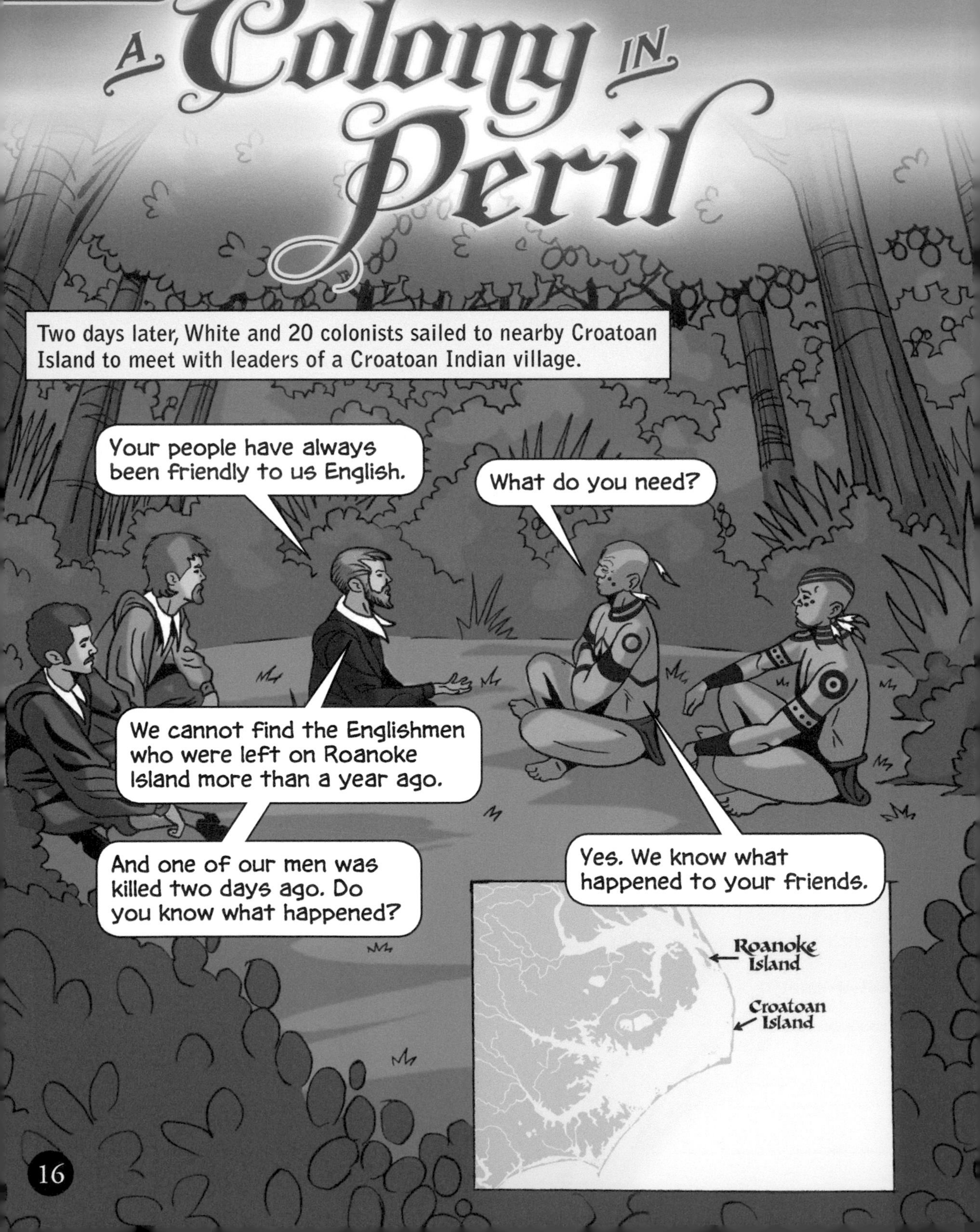
Two days later, White and 20 colonists sailed to nearby Croatoan Island to meet with leaders of a Croatoan Indian village.
Your people have always been friendly to us English.
What do you need?
We cannot find the Englishmen who were left on Roanoke Island more than a year ago.
And one of our men was killed two days ago. Do you know what happened?
Yes. We know what happened to your friends.
Roanoke Island
Croatoan Island

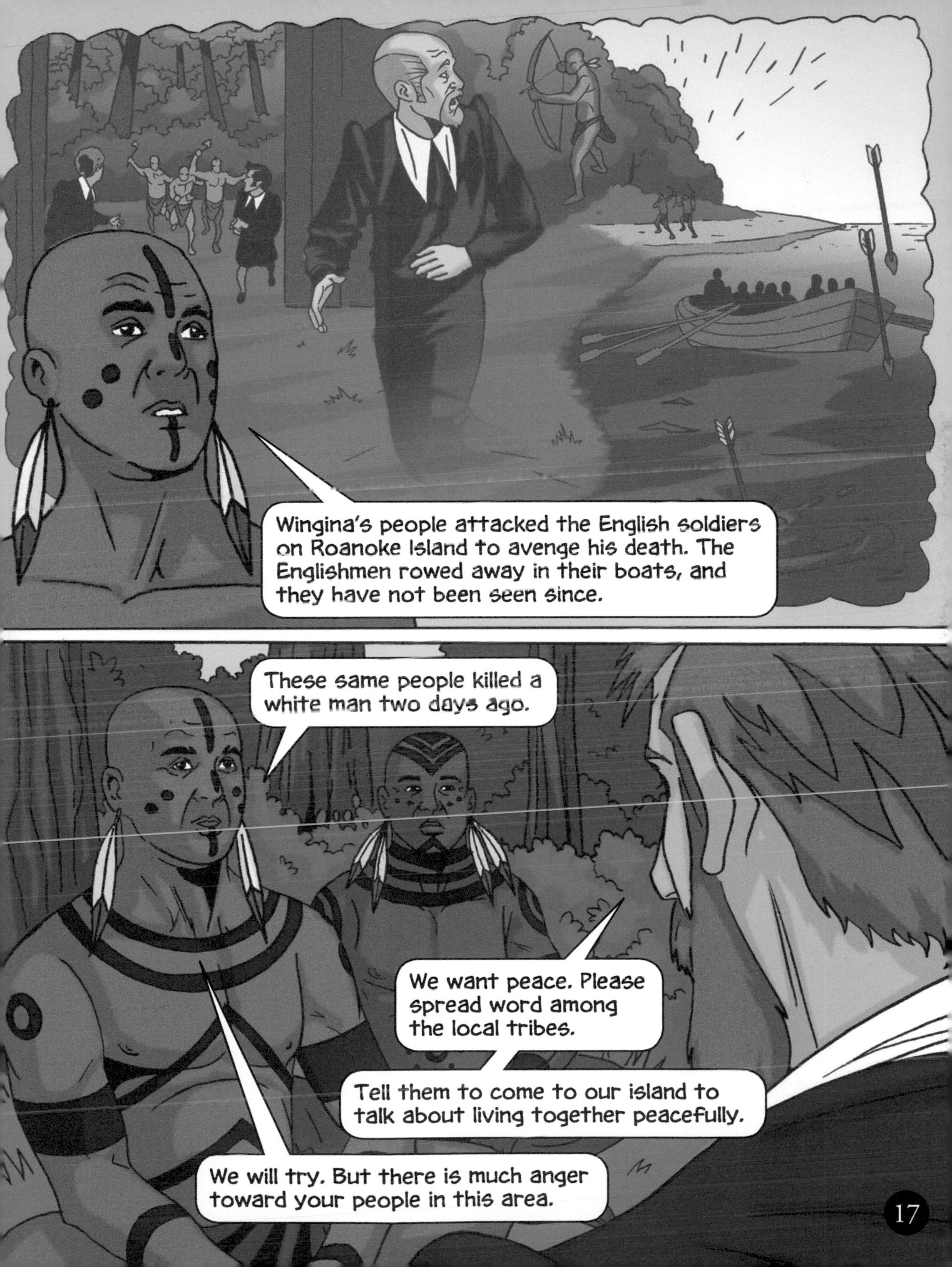
Wingina's people attacked the English soldiers on Roanoke Island to avenge his death. The Englishmen rowed away in their boats, and they have not been seen since.
These same people killed a white man two days ago.
We want peace. Please spread word among the local tribes.
Tell them to come to our island to talk about living together peacefully.
We will try. But there is much anger toward your people in this area.

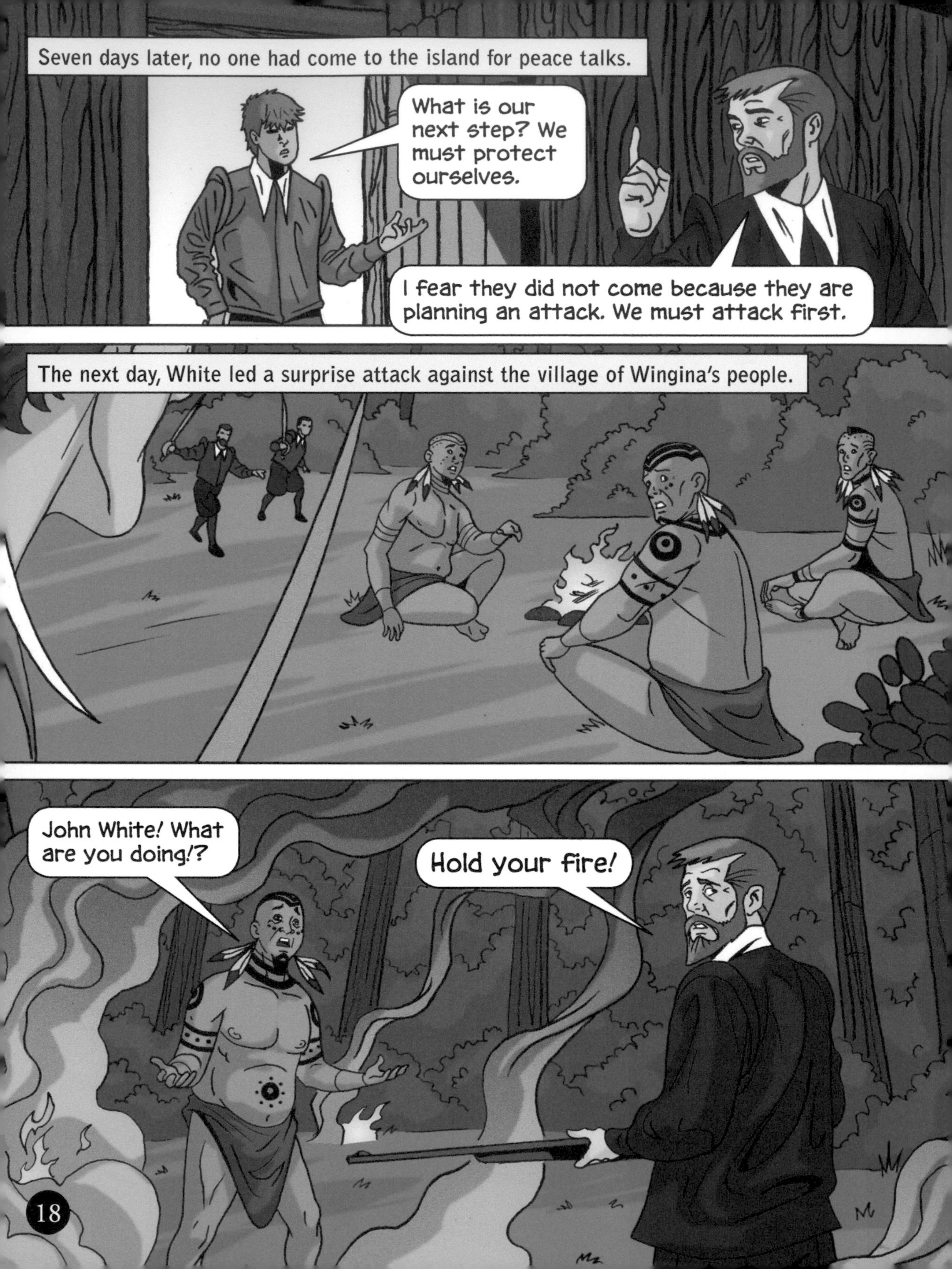
Seven days later, no one had come to the island for peace talks.
What is our next step? We must protect ourselves.
I fear they did not come because they are planning an attack. We must attack first.
The next day, White led a surprise attack against the village of Wingina's people.
John White! What are you doing!?
Hold your fire!

But you are Croatoans, our only friends. Why are you here, in Wingina's village?
We came to tell them about the peace talks, but found the village deserted. We stayed to gather up some corn that was left behind.
We thought you were Wingina's men. Can you ever forgive us?
Two weeks later, on August 18, 1587, Eleanor Dare, White's daughter, gave birth to a baby girl.
I will call her Virginia, to honor this land we call Virginia and our Virgin Queen Elizabeth.
She is the first English baby born on American soil. I just hope she is not the last.

Governor White! We don't have enough food, and we don't have time to grow more before winter.
Governor, we are in danger. You must return to England and beg Sir Walter for help. He'll listen to you.
What? Abandon my post? Leave my family behind? Never!
The next day the colonists met with White.
Father, you must return to England.
You must go. We all agree. We have no other choice.
Very well. I will go to England. I'll be back soon with help.

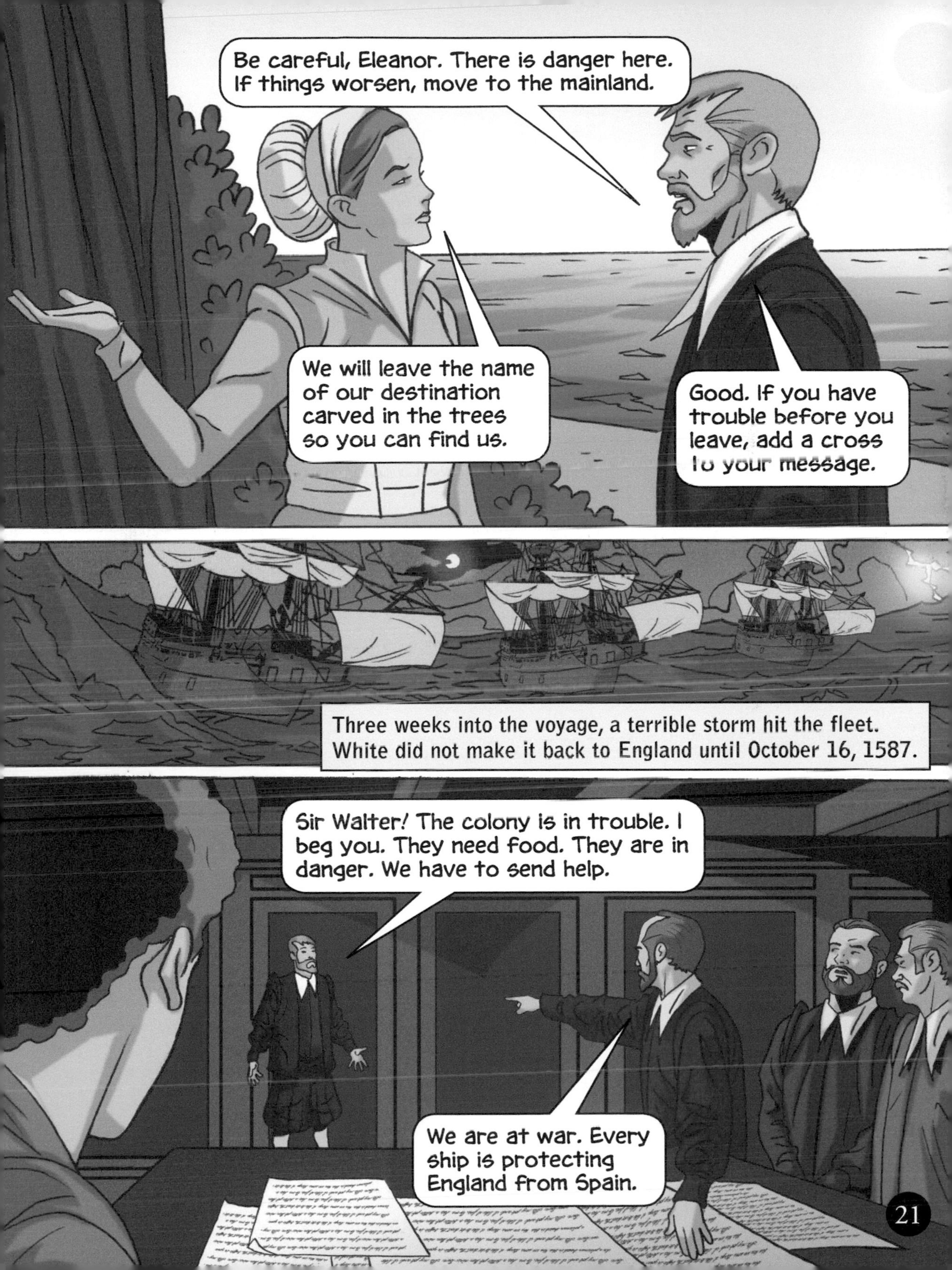
Be careful, Eleanor. There is danger here. If things worsen, move to the mainland.
We will leave the name of our destination carved in the trees so you can find us.
Good. If you have trouble before you leave, add a cross to your message.
Three weeks into the voyage, a terrible storm hit the fleet. White did not make it back to England until October 16, 1587.
Sir Walter! The colony is in trouble. I beg you. They need food. They are in danger. We have to send help.
We are at war. Every ship is protecting England from Spain.

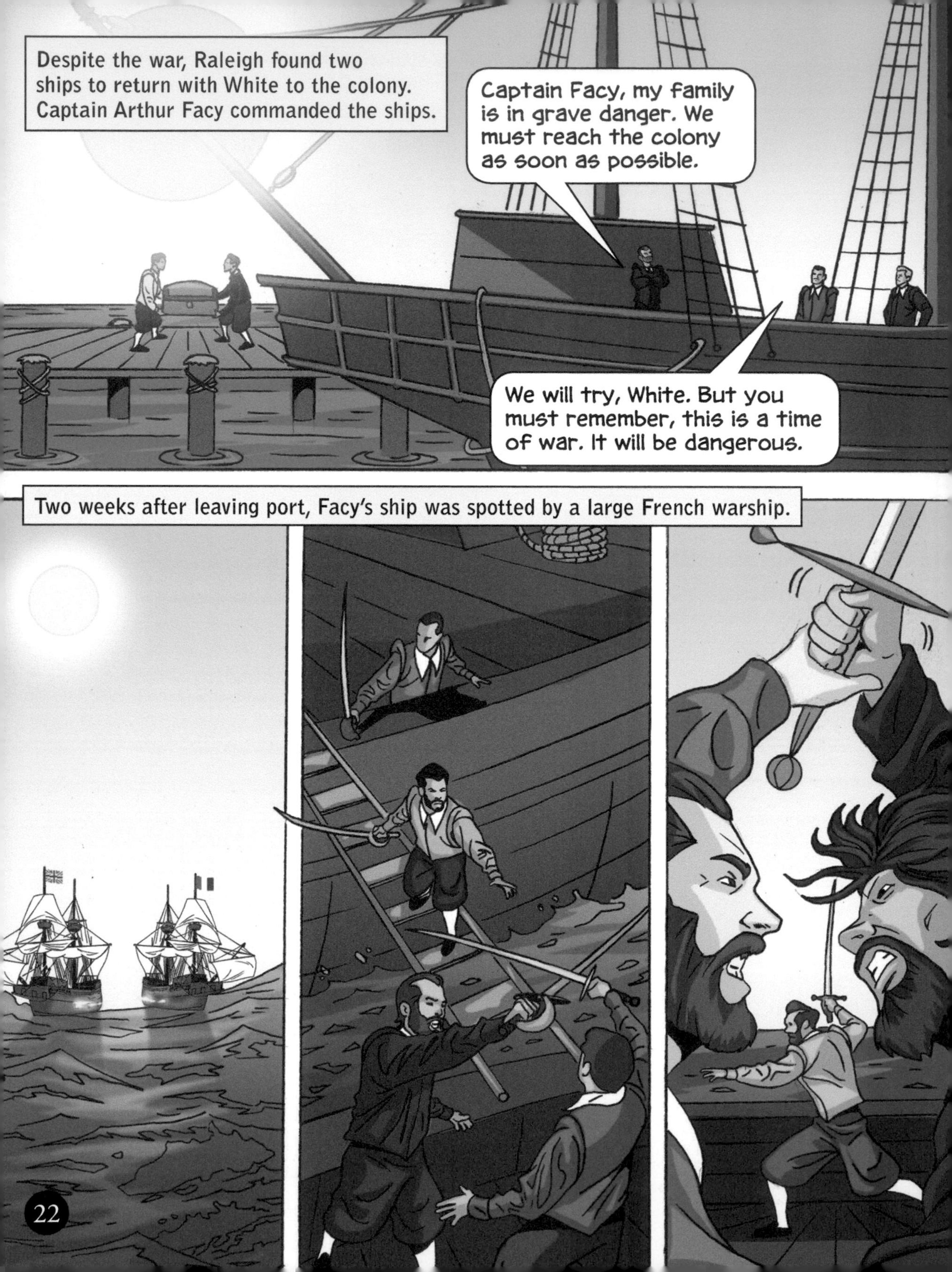
Despite the war, Raleigh found two ships to return with White to the colony. Captain Arthur Facy commanded the ships.
Captain Facy, my family is in grave danger. We must reach the colony as soon as possible.
We will try, White. But you must remember, this is a time of war. It will be dangerous.
Two weeks after leaving port, Facy's ship was spotted by a large French warship.

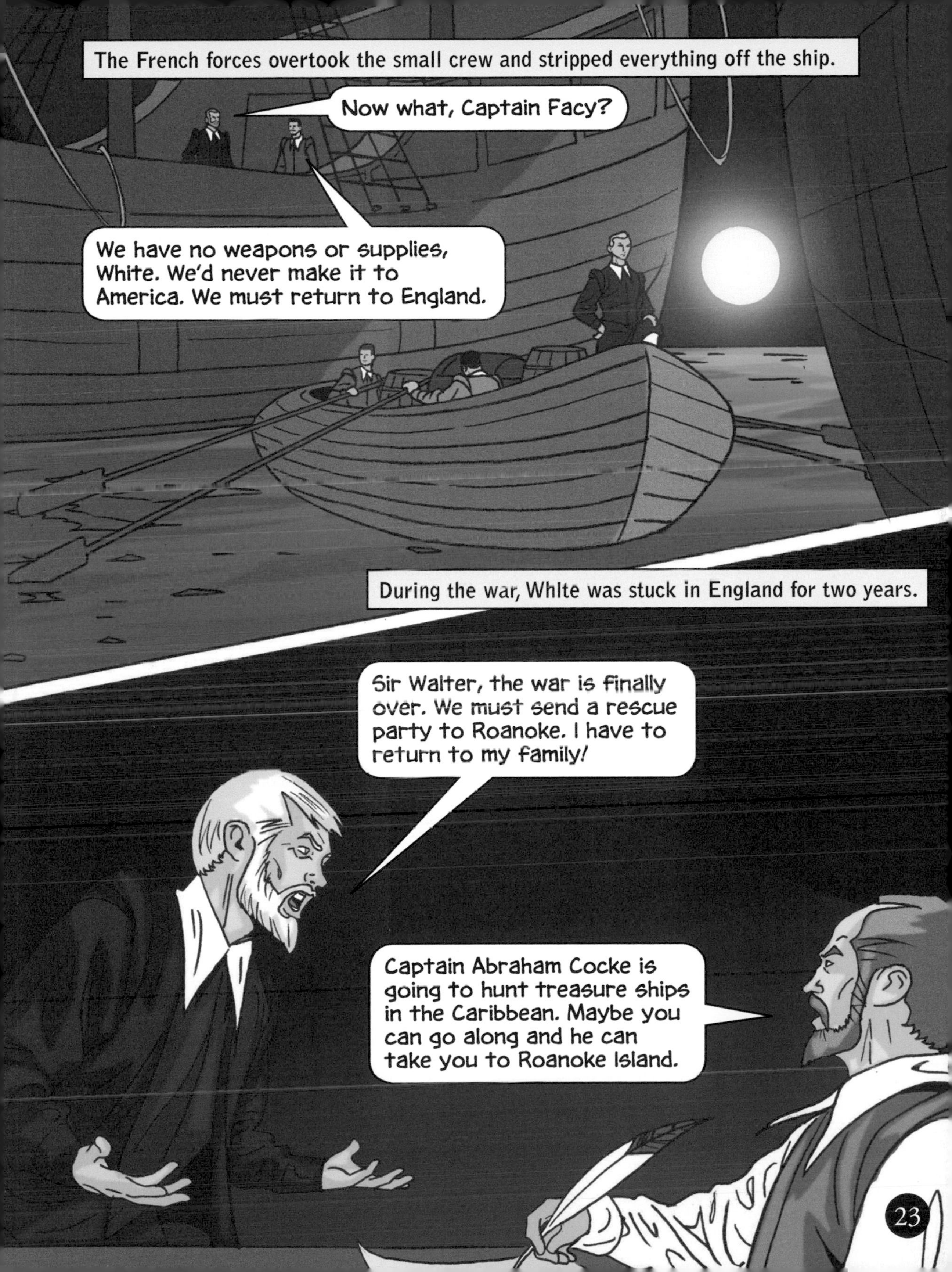
The French forces overtook the small crew and stripped everything off the ship.
Now what, Captain Facy?
We have no weapons or supplies, White. We'd never make it to America. We must return to England.
During the war, White was stuck in England for two years.
Sir Walter, the war is finally over. We must send a rescue party to Roanoke. I have to return to my family!
Captain Abraham Cocke is going to hunt treasure ships in the Caribbean. Maybe you can go along and he can take you to Roanoke Island.

CHAPTER 4

A Colony Lost

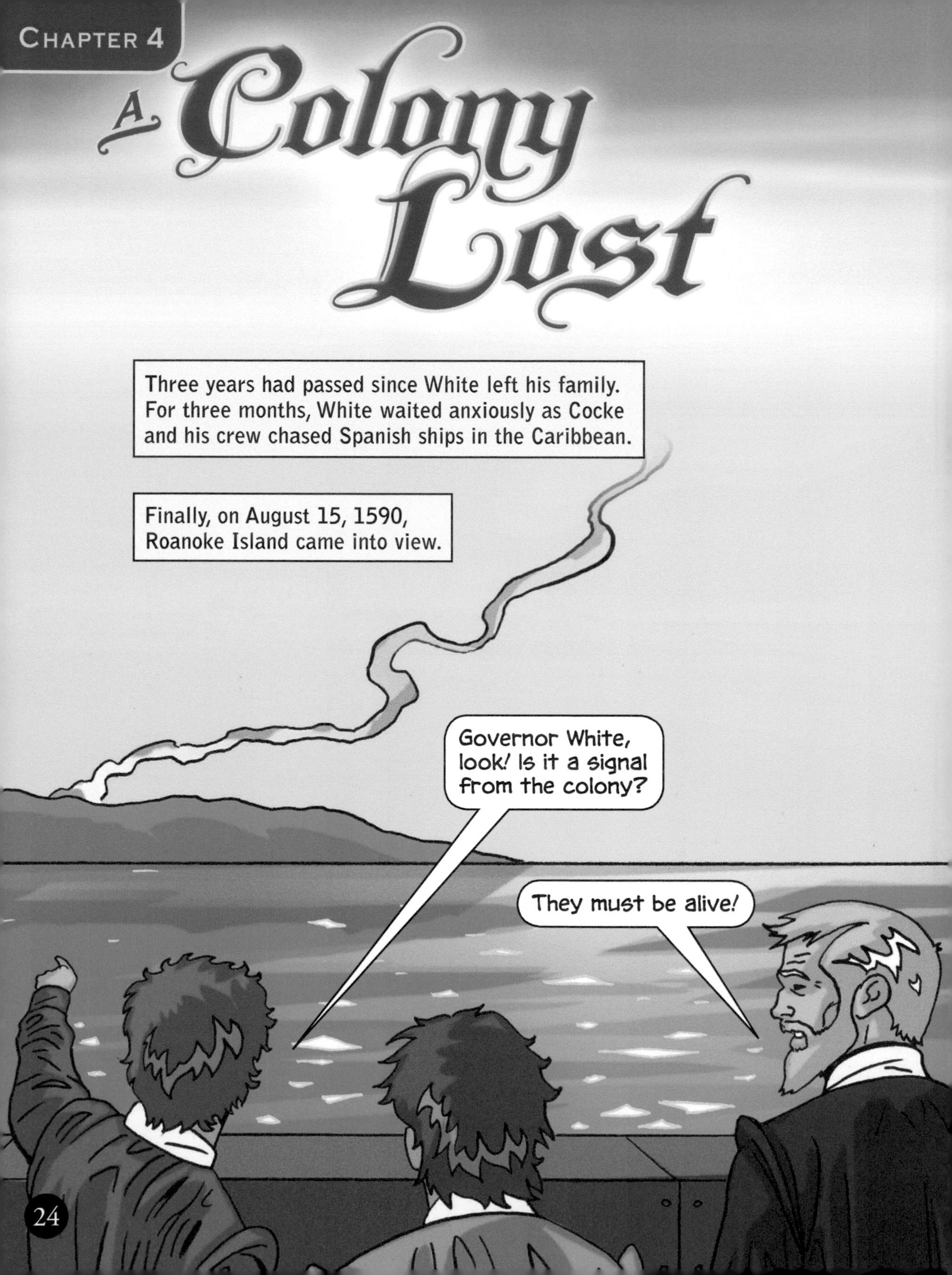
Three years had passed since White left his family. For three months, White waited anxiously as Cocke and his crew chased Spanish ships in the Caribbean.
Finally, on August 15, 1590, Roanoke Island came into view.
Governor White, look! Is it a signal from the colony?
They must be alive!

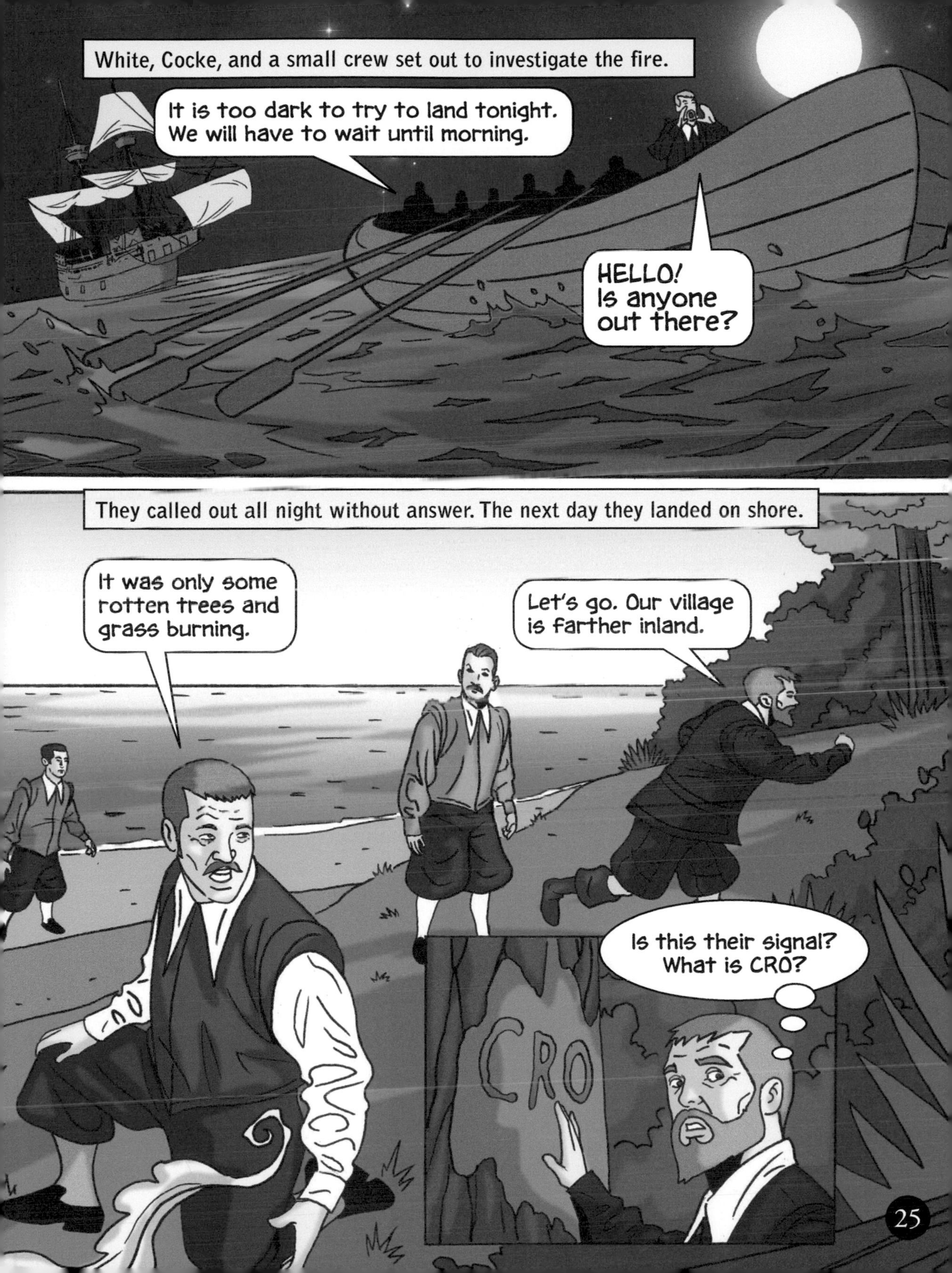
White, Cocke, and a small crew set out to investigate the fire.
It is too dark to try to land tonight. We will have to wait until morning.
HELLO! Is anyone out there?
They called out all night without answer. The next day they landed on shore.
It was only some rotten trees and grass burning.
Let's go. Our village is farther inland.
Is this their signal? What is CRO?
CRO

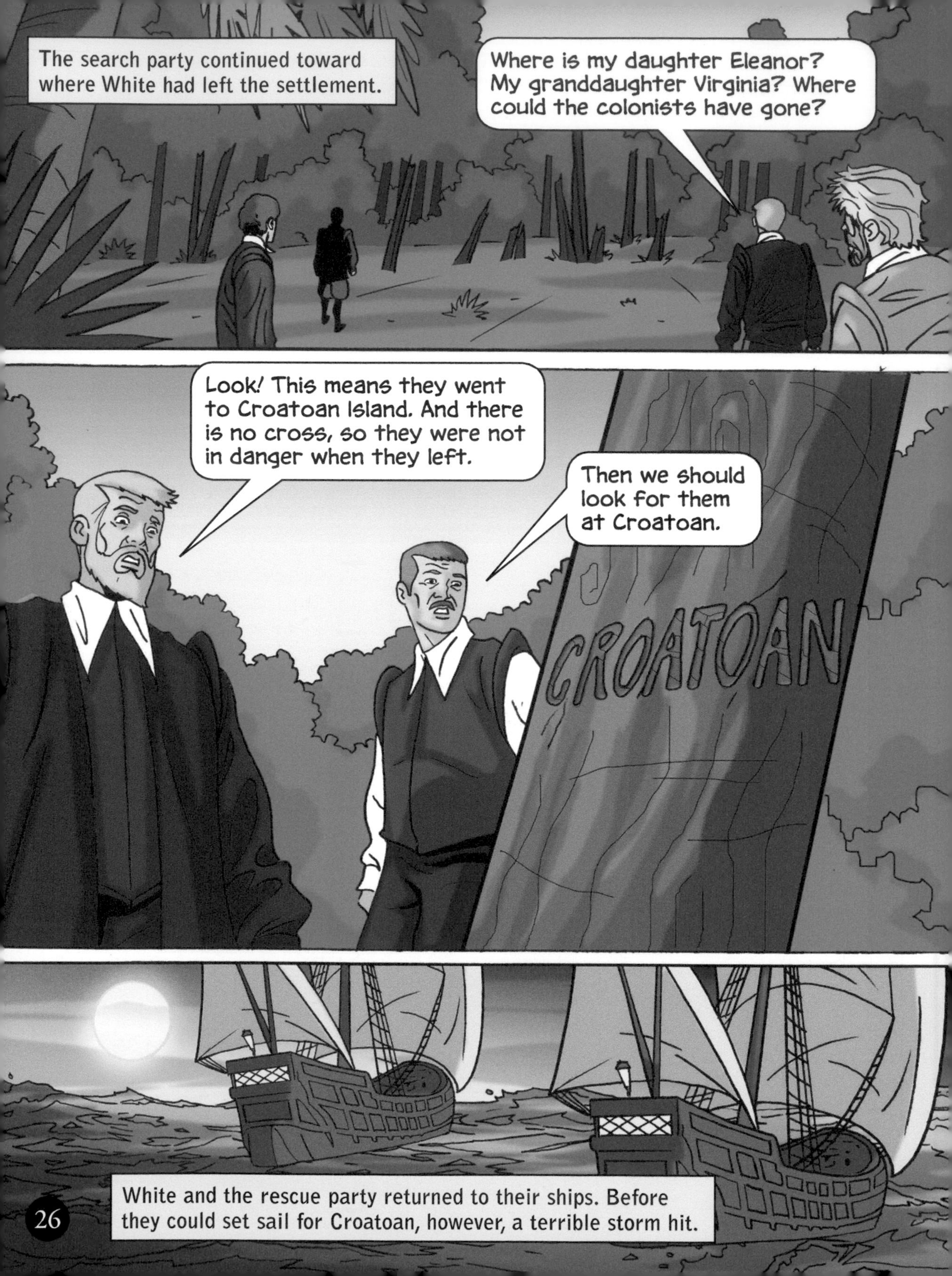
The search party continued toward where White had left the settlement.
Where is my daughter Eleanor? My granddaughter Virginia? Where could the colonists have gone?
Look! This means they went to Croatoan Island. And there is no cross, so they were not in danger when they left.
Then we should look for them at Croatoan.
CROATOAN
White and the rescue party returned to their ships. Before they could set sail for Croatoan, however, a terrible storm hit.

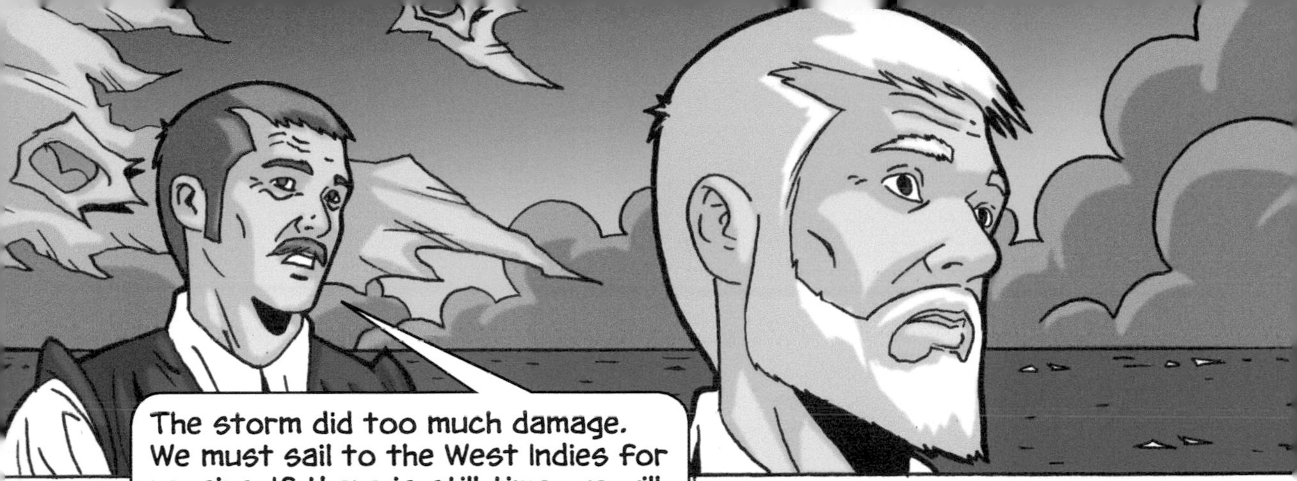
The storm did too much damage. We must sail to the West Indies for repairs. If there is still time, we will return to Croatoan afterwards.

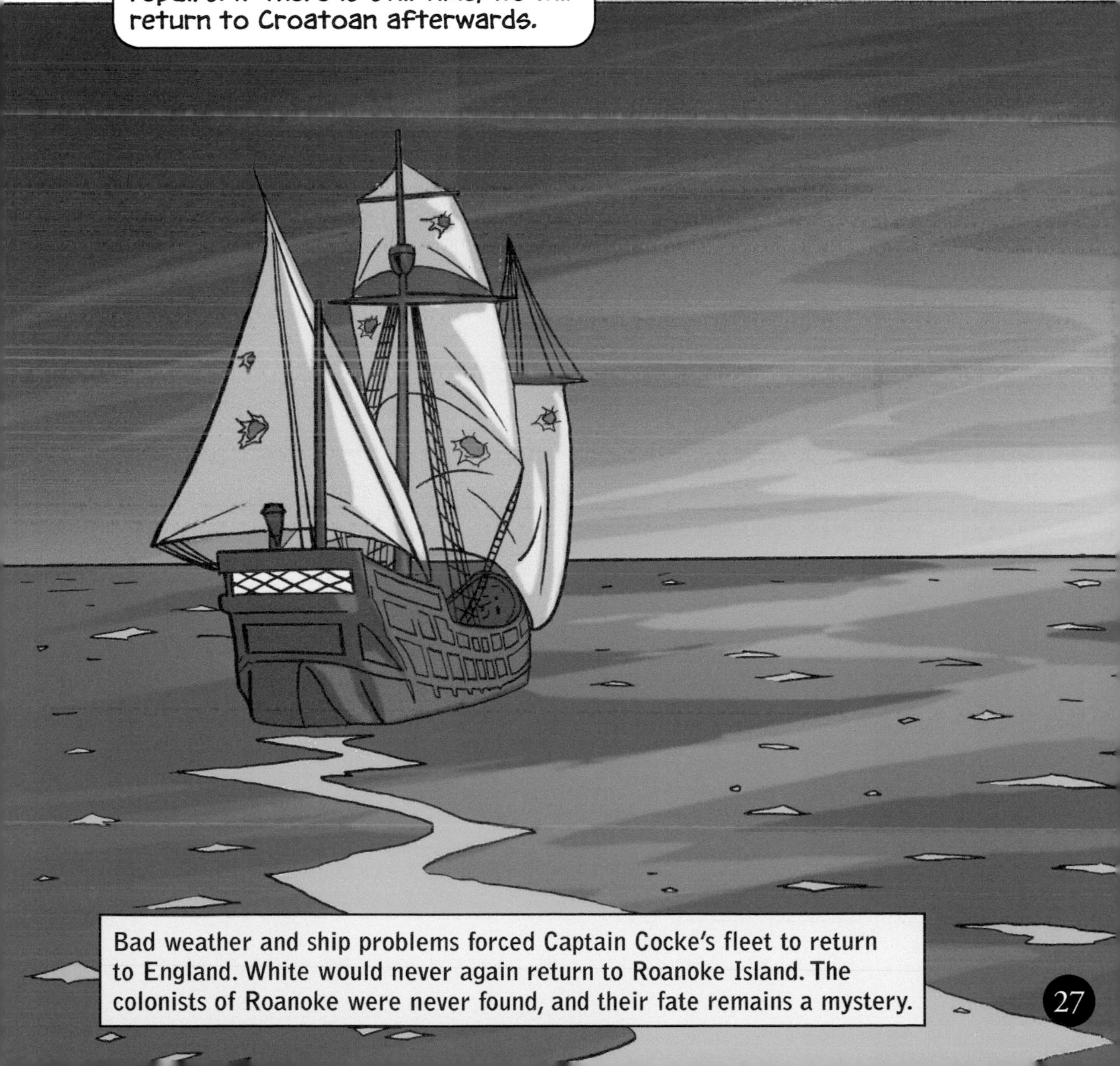
Bad weather and ship problems forced Captain Cocke's fleet to return to England. White would never again return to Roanoke Island. The colonists of Roanoke were never found, and their fate remains a mystery.

More about the Lost Colony

In 1607, England established a permanent settlement in Jamestown, Virginia. In 1608, the governor of Jamestown, John Smith, spoke to the local Indian Chief Powhatan about the Roanoke colonists. Powhatan confessed that during his war with tribes of Chesapeake Bay, his men attacked and killed a group of Europeans that had settled in the area. As proof he showed Smith a musket barrel and a bronze mortar and certain pieces of iron, which had been theirs.

To add to the mystery, other Europeans likely passed through the Roanoke area. Sailing parties may have stopped in the area as they sailed north out of the Caribbean on their way back to Europe. No one ever saw the Roanoke colonists.

The people of Jamestown continued to search for the lost colonists, sending out two expeditions in 1608. Neither of the groups found any physical evidence of the missing colonists. They did bring back rumors of two white men, four white boys, and a white woman working as slaves in a copper mine run by an Indian leader.

- In 1709, surveyor John Lawson reported that the Cape Hatteras and the Croatoan Indians spoke of ancestors who dressed like Europeans and who could read. Lawson also noted that a number of the Croatoans had gray eyes, common in Europeans but rare among Indians.

- Between 1947 and 1950, archaeologists studying Roanoke Island made an unexpected discovery. They found the remains of Lane's fort buried under several layers of dirt. However, they found no evidence of what happened to the missing colonists.

- Today, many historians believe that the colonists left Roanoke Island soon after White's departure and split into two groups. One group went to Croatoan to watch for English ships. A larger group moved north to Chesapeake Bay. There colonists lived alongside a Chesapeake tribe until they were killed by an Indian confederacy under the leadership of Chief Powhatan. This is only a theory, however, and many archaeologists and historians continue to search for the true fate of the lost colony.

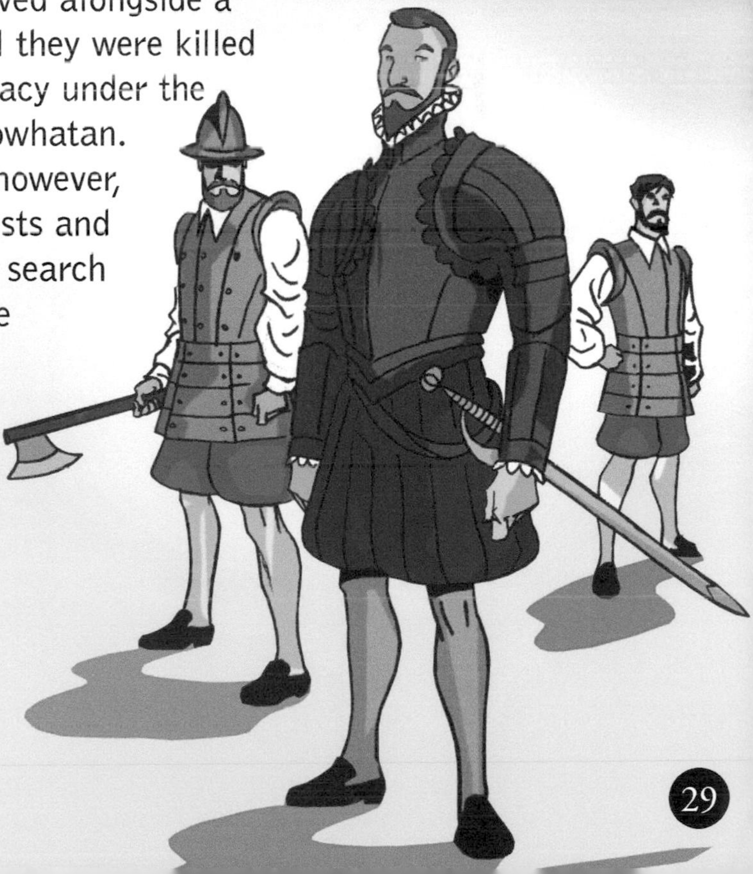

Glossary

abandoned (uh-BAN-duhnd)—deserted or no longer used

assess (uh-SESS)—to judge how good or bad something is

avenge (uh-VENGE)—to get back at someone for hurting you

colony (KOL-uh-nee)—a territory that has been settled by people from another country and is controlled by that country

expedition (ek-spuh-DISH-uhn)—a long journey for a certain purpose, such as exploring

fleet (FLEET)—a group of ships

self-sufficient (SELF suh-FISH-uhnt)—able to take care of one's own needs without help from others

Internet Sites

FactHound offers a safe, fun way to find Internet sites related to this book. All of the sites on FactHound have been researched by our staff.

Here's how:

1. *Visit www.facthound.com*
2. Type in this special code **0736864946** for age-appropriate sites. Or enter a search word related to this book for a more general search.
3. Click on the **Fetch It** button.

FactHound will fetch the best sites for you!

Read More

Dolan, Edward F. *Lost Colony of Roanoke.* New York: Benchmark Books/Marshall Cavendish, 2002.

Fritz, Jean. *The Lost Colony of Roanoke.* New York: G.P. Putnam's Sons, 2004.

Petrie, Kristin. *Sir Walter Raleigh.* Explorers. Edina, Minn.: Abdo, 2006.

Yolen, Jane, and Heidi Elisabet Yolen Stemple. *Roanoke: The Lost Colony: An Unsolved Mystery from History.* New York: Simon & Schuster Books for Young Readers, 2003.

Bibliography

Hakluyt, Richard. *Voyages and Discoveries; The Principal Navigations, Voyages, Traffiques, and Discoveries of the English Nation.* Harmondsworth, England: Penguin, 1972.

Kupperman, Karen Ordahl. *Roanoke, The Abandoned Colony.* Totowa, N.J.: Rowman & Allanheld, 1984.

Miller, Lee. *Roanoke: Solving the Mystery of the Lost Colony.* New York: Arcade, 2001.

Noël Hume, Ivor. *The Virginia Adventure: Roanoke to James Towne: An Archaeological and Historical Odyssey.* Charlottesville: University Press of Virginia, 1997.

Quinn, David B. *Set Fair For Roanoke: Voyages And Colonies, 1584–1606.* Chapel Hill, London: University of North Carolina Press, 1985.

Index